The

Compassion

of

JAZZ

The

Compassion
of
JAZZ

My Incredible Life
in Music &
The Movement

by
Jim Cassell

REGENT PRESS
Berkeley, California

Paperback

ISBN 10: 1-58790-493-4

ISBN 13: 978-1-58790-493-6

E-Book

ISBN 10: 1-58790-494-2

ISBN 13: 978-1-58790t-494-3

Library of Congress Control Number: 2020935499

Most photographs by Jim Cassell.
Several posters by Ruben Guzman.
The others provided anonymously or courtesy of friends
and acquaintances. If additional credit is known and due,
please contact the publisher.

Manufactured in the U.S.A.
REGENT PRESS
Berkeley, California
www.regentpress.net

TABLE OF CONTENTS

CHAPTER 1
The United Farm Workers 9

CHAPTER 2
Pioneers 27

CHAPTER 3
Family & Adolescence 45

CHAPTER 4
Veracruz, Mexico 55

CHAPTER 5
Tripping Out of San Francisco 61

CHAPTER 6
In the Navy Now 69

CHAPTER 7
Off to Work 77

CHAPTER 8
Finding Life's Purpose 85

CHAPTER 9
Cassell/Cibrian Presents 93

CHAPTER 10
The Berkeley Agency 103

CHAPTER 11
America's Music 115

CHAPTER 12
Valerie 129

POSTERS & BUTTONS 135

CHAPTER

1

The United Farm Workers

The United Farm Workers headquarters needed to move from Delano—it was too small, too dusty, and too small-town for such a big movement. Then Cesar heard about a property going up to bid—an old tuberculosis hospital with acres of land surrounding it (some of Cesar's relatives had been treated at the hospital while it had been running). It'd be perfect for the new headquarters, but there was a big issue—it was in the middle of Kern County in the Tehachapi Mountains, which was heavily Republican.

Once it became public knowledge that Cesar and the union were interested in the land, powerful conservatives in Kern County were determined to make sure he didn't get it. A Jewish Hollywood producer who was very sympathetic to La Causa offered to help the union acquire the property. They worked out a plan where Richard Chavez, Cesar Chavez's brother, would dress up like a chauffeur to drive the producer in a limousine to make a bid on the property. After the Hollywood producer won the bid, he turned the land over to Cesar Chavez and the United Farm Workers, outmaneuvering the power brokers of Kern County.

The new headquarters were in Kern, California, and were nicknamed La Paz. It was different, though, in the new center. The beauty of the union was that it felt like one big family, full of love and support and united by our common goal of fighting for a better life for the farmworkers. Now it felt a bit like a monastery—everyone was working all the time, without the previous feeling of camaraderie. That isn't to say it was a bad work environment in the least; every person who worked for the union was a good person. We all worked hard and sacrificed.

When I rejoined the United Farm Workers, I asked Cesar to let me be a photographer, but he said, "No, Jim, I want you to put on more benefits, like you did with Santana," which I had done when their first album came out. Cesar had Joan Baez in mind, as they had a close personal relationship. This is the first concert I put on from scratch, whereas I had had the Fillmore Auditorium's help with the previous Santana benefit.

While I was still planning, Steve Miller called and asked to be a part of the benefit, though I have no idea how he had heard about it. When Steve Miller showed up, he told security he was part of the show and called himself "Stevie Guitar Miller." I am sure the rough-looking chicano security guards didn't believe him at first.

The concert went really well. It was at the San Jose State football stadium, called the Spartan Stadium. Joan Baez headlined, and Steve Miller, Cal Tjader, a teatro group, and a mariachi band played as well. Joan Baez was very gracious and easy to work with. We called the show Fiesta Campesina, and at least 5,000 people came—it was more successful than we had expected. I had spent months putting the show together, and it could never have been done without all the volunteer effort of the community.

People in the printing trades donated hundreds of hours and money to the cause to print the posters, pamphlets, envelopes, etc. The artist of the poster donated his artwork, and the musicians donated their time to put on an unpaid concert; not to mention all the volunteers it took just to run the event. Cesar and his family came up to see the concert and participate in taking tickets and so on. This concert really set me on the path that led to my becoming a music producer later in my life. I greatly enjoyed the independence of setting up concerts with al-

United Farm Workers march from Delano
to Sacramento. (1965)

Cesar Chavez speaking in Sacramento during
the march from Delano.

JOAN BAEZ

Jim's first show after meeting with Cesar was with Joan Baez. Here is the promotional photo that was used.

First UFW concert flyer. (1971)

most full control over all the variables. I was able to work freely from the Bay Area and wasn't required to work out of the headquarters.

The UFW gave me an old red convertible Valiant slant-head six-engine to use as I set up benefit concerts, and I loved that car. Getting artists to commit to playing benefits, often for free or even at their own low expense, took a lot of work and a soft sort of persistence from me. It was a successful strategy, as we were able to make the Fiesta Campesina an annual concert. Every year it was bigger than the last, with a large variety of artists, both musicians and poets alike. I did other benefit concerts during the year when we weren't putting on the Fiesta Campesinas. Over the six years that I worked for the United Farm Workers, I produced over twenty-five benefit concerts with a diverse array of artists such as Santana, Cheech and Chong, Crosby Nash, Rita Coolidge, New Riders of the Purple Sage, John Kahn, Merl Saunders, Mike Bloomfield, Philip Whalen, The Charlatans, Taj Mahal, Pete Escovedo and Sheila E, Coke Escovedo, Dakila, Cal Tjader, Steve Miller, Bola Sete, Toni and Terry from Joy of Cooking, Stone Ground, Dan Hicks, Vince Guaraldi, Joan Baez, Eddie Palmeri, Robert Creeley, Red Wing, Luis Gasca, and El Chicano. We had beatnik poets Allen Ginsburg and Lawrence Ferlingetti, Latino rock stars Jorge Santana and Malo, legendary Tex-Mex artists Little Joe y la Familia, Jerry Garcia of the Grateful Dead, funk-soul musicians Tower of Power, country-western

**Summer in Mariposa. Jim in a UFW convertible given to him
to produce fundraiser shows. (1974)**

singer Kris Kristofferson, and jazz player Eddie Henderson. The poster art for some of these concerts was done by Esteban Villa, who was in the Royal Chicano Airforce, a group of mainly teachers at Sacramento State University who came together and named themselves RCAF as a joke. He often donated his artwork to La Causa, and his paintings were very popular. There were many great posters done by gifted artists, nearly all donated to the UFW.

All the artists I booked were dedicated to *La Causa*. Many other people were interested in supporting the cause, but this was during the Nixon era—community leaders were being bought off by government jobs. We had disdain for those who sold out; they were commonly called "poverty pimps." Unionization was how we were able to protect ourselves, and unions often helped each other out—the International Longshoremen's Union supported the UFW and helped our cause. They, and several other unions as well as religious and ethnic organizations, would organize food caravans to feed the strikers all over California.

In May of 1972, the then governor of Arizona Jack Williams, who was called One-Eyed Jack by the media, made provisions of the Farm Labor Bill which made it next to impossible to strike during harvest times and prohibited secondary boycotts. It was in direct conflict with what the United Farm Workers were trying to do in Arizona, so we did a huge campaign to reverse

One-Eyed Jack's actions and to support his opposition, even bringing in strikers from across the border. The opposing candidate, Jerry Pollock, didn't win, but we were able to drum up a lot of attention to La Causa. I worked in Arizona during the lengthy campaign and did a big benefit concert with Little Joe y la Familia, which raised a lot of money and publicity for the union.

I worked for the union for six years, from 1969 to 1975, putting on concerts and benefits and doing all the organizational work that they entailed. Though I believed wholeheartedly in the work the union was doing and still does to this day, I was feeling less and less dedicated as the years went on—I was burning out. Toward the end of my time with the United Farm Workers, I felt the UFW board wanted to control me more, to churn out more concerts than I feasibly could.

The pressure of constantly getting artists to perform for free was starting to wear on me. In 1975, the Board of Directors (Cesar Chavez, Richard Chavez, Dolores Huerta, Philip Veracruz, Pete Velasco, etc.) didn't okay the project I was working on. I proposed to put on a fairly typical concert at the Sonoma State athletic field with Kris Kristofferson, Rita Coolidge, Taj Mahal, and others. The board questioned the whole show and called me down to La Paz to meet with the board. I felt let down, after all the successful benefits I had done and money and publicity I had raised, to not be trusted with this project.

I took it as a sign that the time to leave the United

Farm Workers had come, so I sent Cesar a resignation letter in which I thanked him for the opportunity to work for the UFW but stated that it was time for me to go. I wished them the best of luck, and I will always be a supporter of the United Farm Workers. Years later, Dolores Huerta would occasionally ask me to come back and do concerts after I left, but I had already moved on. I will always be grateful for my time with the union and with Cesar—he was the one who steered me into producing concerts for a living, when I had originally planned to be a photographer. Working for the union was a, if not the, highlight of my life.

UNITED FARM WORKERS
ORGANIZING COMMITTEE, AFL-CIO

CESAR CHAVEZ
Director
LARRY ITLIONG
Asst. Director

P.O. Box 62
Keene, Ca. 93531
(805) 822-5571

March 9, 1972

To Whom It May Concern:

JIM CASSELL is authorized to represent the United
Farm Workers. He is further impowered to do fund-
raising activities on behalf of the Union. I will
appreciate whatever help you can give to him.
With our spreading organizational activities, we
continue to need to draw financial help from the
general public and we look forward to the help
you will be in this way.

Most sincerely,

Cesar E. Chavez,
Director

ssd

**Letter from Cesar Chavez authorizing Jim to represent the
United Farm Workers and do fund raising. (1972)**

19

**Marchers cooling off in an irrigation ditch during the
Coachella March from Coachella Valley to Calixico to protest
workers being brought in to break the strike. (1972)**

Jim resting during the Coachella March. (1972)

Undercover police officers are seen here at the end of the
march. Ted Kennedy was also there, as well as many
notables from Los Angeles.

Jim and Roberto Garcia. Salinas Valley. (1973)

Dr. Ralph Abenathy at the UFW protest march,
Coachella Valley.

Caesar Chavez and Bobby Seale, Oakland. (1974)

Rambling Jack Elliot and Kris Kristofferson at a UFW benefit
concert at the Berkeley Greek Theater. (1974)
Kris was a real sweetheart and paid his whole band
himself to show up and perform.

Jim Cassell

**Jim while working with the United Farm Workers (UFW).
(1976)**

CHAPTER

2

Pioneers

y grandfather, Dr. Edward Howard, was from Cornwall, England, and sailed steerage to Massachusetts in 1890 in his teenage years. He was a gifted student, having previously studied in Europe before immigrating, and received a scholarship from the Borden family, of Borden Dairy, to attend Harvard Medical School. He settled in in La Jolla, California, with my grandmother, Eliza Berryman Howard, where he spent the rest of his life as a doctor.

**Jim's grandfather Dr. Edward Howard,
an early La Jolla pioneer, with his mother. (1914)**

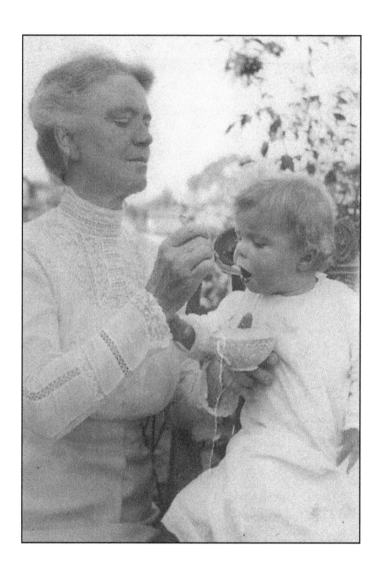

Jim's Grandmother with his mother.

Though his specialty was in childhood diseases, La Jolla was a very small town, and my grandfather served in a greater capacity as the town doctor. He was also the first doctor in La Jolla, and so became a pillar of the community. He was known for his generosity in the seacoast village; when the ranchers, farmers, and regular folk couldn't afford their medical bills, my grandfather accepted eggs and produce as payment—he never turned anyone away. In fact, in the 1970s, Cliff Robertson wrote my mother a letter in which he describes his grandmother telling him of how my grandfather could be seen in his backyard burning the medical bills of families who couldn't pay.

He prevented an unknowable number of drownings by putting up lifesaving rings along the beaches. However, Dr. Howard was not good with money. During the Great Depression, he made some bad investments, and eventually he and Eliza needed to sell their three little houses, known as the "Oleander," the "Geranium," and the "Columbine." They moved to a little apartment in San Diego, where they lived until their deaths.

Before moving, my grandmother Eliza had just as lasting an impact on La Jolla as Dr. Howard. She was a pillar of the community in her own right. She planted the ice plants along the shore, which flourish to this day. She was the president of the Women's Club of La Jolla, which was housed in a beautiful mission-style building with surrounding gardens. She also worked closely with

Jim's maternal grandmother (circled) was in the first graduating class of women at Colorado State University.

Mrs. Scripps, heiress of the Scripps newspaper dynasty who retired in La Jolla, to build the Scripps Institute of Oceanography, the Episcopal Church of St. James-by-the-Sea, the Scripps Hospital, and the children's pool.

My grandmother was one of the twelve students to graduate from Colorado Teachers College in 1890, notable for being the first graduating class of that college to include women. Before meeting my grandfather, she had worked as a schoolteacher in Glenwood Springs, Colorado, where she enjoyed the natural beauty of the Rockies. Living up there had its dangers, particularly mountain lions.

My mother told me the story of a pelt my grandmother had, and the story of how she came to have it: she had been walking home alone along the trails from the schoolhouse at dusk one day, and, upon reaching a bluff, noticed a mountain lion stalking her. She looked around for help and could only see some far-off farmhands pitching hay in a field, so she lifted her skirts and waved them frantically to get their attention. One farmhand waved back, oblivious to the danger, but luckily the other saw the mountain lion and rushed off for his shotgun.

Essentially, Eliza Howard was a progressive, liberated woman for her time, and her viewpoints and experiences greatly affected how she raised my mother, and in turn how my mother raised me. My mother told me a story from when she was young, when she once made fun of a black woman walking in front of her house. Her mother overheard her comments and yanked my mom out of the house by the ear, giving her a stern talking to about discrimination.

Both my grandparents taught my mom to be generous to those with little money, and to never be cruel on the basis of race and color. While La Jolla wasn't the most diverse town, it had a Hispanic district, an African American district, and a small Filipino presence as well as the white middle class. My mother, Victoria "Bicky" Howard, always said that it was her mother who taught her to have empathy, especially toward minorities, which she made sure to impart to her own children.

Dr. Howard and Eliza Howard were not my mother's biological parents—they adopted her when she was a toddler. Her biological father was Gildas Charles Evans,

Jim's biological grandfather, Gildas Evans, who had to put his daughter (Jim's mom) up for adoption after his wife died.

who came over from South Wales. He was a good-look-
ing, musically minded man, and he made his money by
teaching singing and giving instrument lessons. He met
and married Ethel May Cool, and they arrived in La Jolla
in 1900. Ethel died in childbirth, leaving Gildas with my
newborn mother and his grief. In 1914, he gave my mother up for adoption to Dr. Howard and Eliza, who were in
their sixties at the time. My mother only found out about
her adoption many years later, when she was a teenager
overhearing some cruel comments from schoolmates.

I was born in 1945 in La Jolla, where I spent the
first ten marvelous years of my life. Back then, I went by
a different name: Corky Cassell. My mom had seen the
name in a listening booth in a record store—it was writ-
ten as graffiti on the walls. What was obvious to her was
that Corky was a character—he had long hair, walked all
summer barefoot, and had a kind of "surfer kid" attitude
to him. My mom thought it was a fun name, and thus
nicknamed me. She was right to foresee the importance
of the beach in my life, as I would quickly come to define
myself by the ocean.

La Jolla was not a wealthy town, but it was rich
in natural beauty, being situated on an outcropping of
California just north of San Diego. Meaning "the jewel"
in Spanish, the village lived up to its sparkling name in a
National Geographic spread in 1952. The ocean faces the
town on three sides, and still is the main source of en-
tertainment for the residents. I learned to walk alongside

learning to swim with a baby's instinctive dogpaddling skill, and my mother would frequently take us to the beach to play and to explore the cathedral-like caves nearby. We would go cliff diving and snorkeling regularly, and every day was a magical adventure of one kind or another.

My mother, when she was young, would climb up Mount Soledad, which has a lovely cross at the peak, and pick wildflowers. During the summers, however, I was on my own, as my mom struggled to support three children by herself, working retail and later as a dental assistant. It was a small town, and people knew each other's business and conditions, and were generous to us. A friend lent us a car, others gave us their hand-me-downs, as well as other acts of kindness. In particular, I remember a lifeguard, Dick Soper, who was something of a father figure to me in those early years. He would pitch in and buy me some lunch sometimes, as he knew I didn't always have money.

My biological father, who I was named after, had left when I was young, and Dick stepped into the role, teaching me about the beauty of the ocean but also the adventures that could be had at the cove beach. I would go snorkeling in the gorgeous reefs and swim through the eel grass that grew there.

My biological father had little in common with his own father, Harrison Howard Cassell, who died before I was born. Harrison put himself through law school and

became the district attorney of Los Angeles, leading re-
lief efforts in the wake of an earthquake in Mexico, and
even running for the Senate. After his divorce from my
paternal grandmother, who I only ever knew as Nana, he
became an alcoholic and died poor in a boarding house.
My nana was a Christian Scientist. Christian Science
doesn't believe in doctors, and she died when I was
three years old. My father, Jim Cassell, did not reach the
career heights my grandfather did, but both constantly
battled alcoholism throughout their lives. He didn't have
the initiative to make anything of himself because he
knew he was to inherit upon the death of his mother.
Before or during World War II, my biological father became an alcoholic like his father before him; unfortunately, that's all I really know of him, except that he was
sixty-one years old when he passed away.

I had two siblings then: Mike, who was six years my
senior, and Vicky, who was two years my senior. Mike and
I were not terribly close; he was a distant sort of presence
in my childhood, having been sent to military school when
I was young. He also spent more time with our alcoholic
and abusive father than either Vicky or I did, which sepa-
rated us from him early on. Vicky was my protector, beat-
ing up the kids who bullied me, though she did sometimes
beat me up herself as well. My mom didn't want Vicky to
fight other boys, so she would let us fight out our issues.
I remember the first time I was able to beat my sister was
when I was 12, and after that, the fights tapered off.

La Jolla was a small town when my grandparents settled, consisting mostly of ranches, farms, and regular folk. It attracted artsy people, dreamers, and those who just wanted to get away from the cold, and thus it quickly grew, having a population of almost 10,000 by the time we moved away. I loved the horses and the hayrides, and had a fondness for "cowboy music" as I knew it. If asked, I would have said that Frankie Lane was my favorite singer, as he sang all the famous Western titles such as "High Noon" and "3:10 to Yuma." I dreamed of having such a ranch once I was grown, a dream no doubt heavily influenced by the movie Westerns I loved. I quickly changed my mind, however, when I learned that scorpions and rattlesnakes were native to Tucson, Arizona, which was the premier place to have a ranch in my young mind. Overall, I was a positive child, with childhood dreams. The first ten years of my life passed in idyllic happiness, and if my mother hadn't remarried, I likely would have grown up to be a lifeguard or a surfer. Growing up in La Jolla was all about having friends and support for me and my mom, helping us get along—it was an embodiment of the saying "it takes a village to raise a child."

Jim's Mom. (1929)

Jim with his Mom — La Jolla. (1946)

Jim (Corky) with his birth dad Jim. (1946)

Jim's siblings, Vicky and Mike. (1947)

Jim (center), Vicky, and Mike. (1947)

Jim at the beach in La Jolla. (1947)

Jim pre-surfing on La Jolla shores. (1951)

CHAPTER

3

Family & Adolescence

y mother met Frank Plaisted during World War II, and were great friends for many years. After my mother's divorce and Frank's wife's death, they married in 1954. Frank and his late wife had adopted Donna, who was a year my junior, and so Mike, Vicky, and I gained an adopted stepsister, and I was no longer the baby of the family.

In 1955 the six of us moved to San Carlos into a "safe" white neighborhood. It was a sterile, suburban sort of place, nice enough but lacking in flavor and substance, and I insisted to my parents that La Jolla was my first

Jim's stepfather Frank Plaisted. (1972)

**Frank, Victoria, Mike, Jim, Vickie, and Donna outside
their home in San Carlos. (1960)**

love, and as soon as I turned eighteen, I would return. In San Carlos, the ocean was no longer a large part of my life—the water was colder, for one thing, and life with my stepfather was much more structured than before.

My stepfather instilled in me a work ethic which I have benefited from my whole life. The dynamic between us as siblings also changed, with Mike being in the army and with the addition of Donna, who was very different from what we were used to. Donna was spoiled and just different from us, and didn't seem accustomed to the sort of roughhousing and fighting that Vicky and I did. The three of us were never especially close, but we got along all right. The house was far from empty—we had exchange students with the American Field Service, one of whom was Maryse Tonelle, a Parisian high school senior who stayed with us for a year when I was thirteen.

Maryse seemed more advanced than us Americans, more sophisticated and mature. Our mothers remained close after that year was up, and I too kept in contact with Maryse, and she went on to become a lawyer and later a judge in France.

When I was eleven, I joined the Boy Scouts of America and was incredibly invested in it. I had been a Cub Scout since the age of six; I found the Boy Scouts to be much more demanding, and I enthusiastically earned many badges, including the God and Country badge and my Eagle Scout badge, pictured on the right.

Eagle Scout Award.

I remember the flare of pride I felt seeing President Eisenhower wearing our Boy Scout neckerchief during the 1960 National Jamboree, which was an incredible experience in and of itself, seeing all those different cultures and people in one place. It was the first time I heard steel drums, played by a Caribbean Boy Scout troop, and the sound stayed with me for years. I played trombone when I was a child, but an accident that shattered my teeth put a stop to that.

I was heavily involved in the church, being the head of the Episcopal Young Churchmen for the dioceses of California at The Good Shepherd Church. We were involved in a work project at True Sunshine Mission in Chinatown in San Francisco, where we painted the walls and learned about Chinese culture. We also went to a very memorable Episcopal camp in the Russian River area every summer. I remember our Welsh pastor Father Daly's beautiful voice singing during the service, and how moved I was. I missed the ocean something fierce, but I had these pursuits to fill the space it left in my life, though it wasn't quite the same.

Eventually I was able to reconnect to the ocean, thanks to my Aunt Thursa in La Jolla. She was an interesting woman of many hobbies and vocations, including Cub Scout master, war correspondent, and cook for the Oregon wagon train reenactment that got pictures in *Look* magazine. Most importantly, she owned a beautiful 90-ft classic schooner called *The Destiny*. It had been built by Howard Hughes in 1934 with a cruising range of 2,000 miles when under power, and was the sister ship of Sterling Hayden's *The Wanderer*, though it had its own claim to fame with its appearance on the television series *Adventures in Paradise*. The captain, Tex, was almost as colorful as Aunt Thursa, being a wrangler from Nevada and the trail boss on the Oregon wagon train reenactment with my aunt. When I was thirteen, they took me on a two-and-a-half-week sailing trip from Sausalito, California, to Portland, Oregon, with stops in Shelter Cove, Coos Bay, Astoria, and up the Columbia River. The first several days of the trip saw horrible foggy weather,

Two-week trip Aunt Thursa's boat. (1960)

with twelve- to twenty-foot swells, and I was constantly seasick, able to only fantasize about eating. Despite the miserable conditions, we still had to do four-hour lookout shifts, and I would sing sea shanties and daydream a lot while I was at the helm. After two or three days, I finally got my sea legs, and at the end of the inclement weather, we pulled into Shelter Cove and repaired the boat. After that we had the Puta Gorda passage to sail around, which is infamous for being very difficult and dangerous. The weather stayed clear and placid, however, and we went through without incident.

As we sailed up the Columbia River, I felt as one with nature and all her moods—the rough weather at night, the flat smoothness of the mornings. I would lie down on the bowsprit and watch the emerald sea glide by. When we arrived in Coos Bay, a local paper did a story on *The Destiny* and our passage. It was a life-changing experience for me to be on the sea I loved so dearly, to learn how to become part of it. The journey reaffirmed what I already knew: that the ocean was in my blood, and I would always need to return to it in my life.

When I was twelve years old, my mother introduced me to another facet of life that ended up becoming a core aspect of who I am: my love of jazz. She was a part-time jazz benefit producer for the Children's Home Society and a musician herself, and she had gone to the very first Monterey Jazz Festival, in 1958, where she saw Billie Holiday perform.

She gave me my first records: Dave Brubeck's *Jazz Impressions of Eurasia* and Oscar Brown Jr.'s *Sin & Soul*. I remember falling in love with Vince Guaraldi's *Cast Your Fate to the Wind* and Cal Jader's Latin jazz sound. Jazz was my ticket to experiencing new places and cultures, something I was desperate for, after having lived in a white suburban neighborhood south of San Francisco. I wanted to keep in touch with the world, and jazz was my way to do it.

I went to the Monterey Jazz Festival for the first time in 1959 and continued to go for the next ten years or so. The festival wasn't exactly welcomed by the city of Monterey at the time, mostly because jazz wasn't respected as a sophisticated art form yet, and not understood

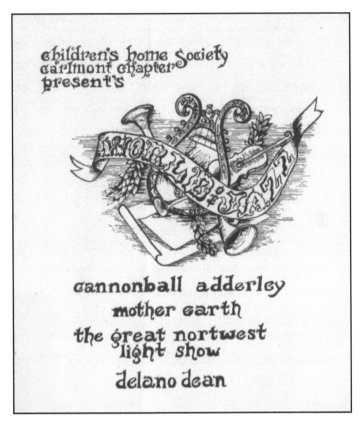

**Poster for a benefit jazz concert produced by Jim's Mom
Vickie for the Children's Home Society. (1968)**

by "the squares." This caused the jazz community to knit
together tightly to worship jazz, and there were times
I felt it was almost like a cult, but a good cult. Even so,
the support and love the racially diverse community had
for jazz was partly why it was so intense and influential
in my life. I'll always remember how surreal that first
Jazz Festival was for me—the thick fog of the September

skies, the greenness of the sweet grass, the beauty of the ancient oak trees, the diversity of the jazz-lovers in the audience and on stage, the magic of hearing music dependent on the energies of the audience and the improvisations of the bands, the connection we all had in those moments that would never be repeated. It was not unlike being really high, and the music would take us on a rollercoaster ride with the artists reaching certain peaks that just can't be replicated. Later in my life, I ended up representing some of these same great artists I saw play at the Monterey Jazz Festival, such as Dizzy Gillespie, Dave Brubreck and Sons, Tito Puente, and many, many more.

CHAPTER

Veracruz, Mexico

The summer of 1963, between my junior and senior years of high school, I was accepted into the Experiment in International Living exchange-student program and was assigned a family in Veracruz, Mexico. I took the train alone for the first time in my life, traveling all over Mexico before returning home, and the sudden independence and responsibility I had suited me. I got my train ticket at the end of June, went down to Union Station in Los Angeles, caught the train through El Paso (where I stepped off for just a little bit; I still remember the boiling hot dry air blistering my skin) to Dallas, Texas, for the orientation. About 120 students, all going to different areas of Mexico, attended the orientation at the University of Houston, and we were all electric with excitement. While in Dallas, I visited my aunt Pat Cassell, her husband Joe, and their children for a short while. It was the 4th of July, and the family was active in the John Birch Society. I wasn't very political at the time, but I was religious, and I found some of the attitudes very shocking. My aunt and uncle wanted my help setting up a float for the parade, and I remember hearing some very unkind sermons at a barbecue from some Pentecostal ministers. Earlier that year, Adlai Stevenson, who was the United Nations Ambassador at the time, was hit with a placard on a visit to Dallas. He was a progressive democrat who had run for president, and the next fall, President Kennedy was assassinated. It was my first glimpse at the political unrest that would soon come to my attention. It was a very toxic time in Dallas, and hate speeches were frequently aired on the local radios.

Eager to move on to Mexico, I quickly left Dallas and took the train south. I relished the freedom to explore a new culture and location, to hear the music played, though I did bring three jazz albums with me: Cal Tjader's *Contemporary Music of Mexico and Brazil*, Dizzy Gillespie's *On the Riviera*, and Dave Brubeck's *Time Further Out*. Although I brought those pieces of home with me, I soaked in every bit of Mexican culture I could while I was there, and I was in a uniquely wonderful place to do it. Veracruz is one of the oldest cities in the

Jim and a friend dancing at the Hotel Mocambo during his exchange summer in Veracruz. "Cuba Libre Time." (1963)

Americas. The beautiful pastel buildings were designed to let the hot, humid air move freely through them so the city seems to breathe with the winds, and the dirt floors of the houses blend the division of outside and inside so I never felt I was kept away from nature, or nature from me. I would go to old colonial hotels, particularly the Hotel Mocambo, to attend the *bailes* they had in the ballrooms, where I drank a lot of *cuba libres* with my Mexican brothers in the hot humid air. I didn't really speak Spanish when I left home, but around three weeks in, once the language flowed into my dreams, I knew I was starting to learn it.

I lived with the Pavóns for this time: Dr. Antonio Pavón, who specialized in children's parasitic disease, the *Señora*, and their children Tonio, Jorge, Danilo, and Gabriel. I liked them all very much and felt very welcome in their home. I felt I wanted to be Mexican; I longed for the affection showed in the family, especially between sons and fathers. They hugged and put their arms around friends and family with casual ease, something I had not experienced. The open display of love was new to me, but I soon felt more at home with it than I could have imagined.

Overall, the experience was incredible. Veracruz was an ancient port city and seemed to me like the Havana of Mexico. I was loath to leave. But I had to return to San Carlos in time for my senior year of high school. This was a big turning point in my young life—I was no longer in the Eagle Scouts or an acolyte in the church. My parents were living in an apartment, and Vicky and Mike had both moved out. I felt I had matured a lot during my summer away, and I chafed against the sudden lack of independence I had once I returned home. Having explored some of the world on my own, high school was too small and narrow in scope to keep my attention; I felt I had outgrown it.

My grades plummeted as a result, but I couldn't bring myself to care very much, as I felt I had already graduated that summer in Mexico, and this year was just a waste of my time before I could move on to more interesting things. The consequence was that one of the only colleges I could get into was Colorado State University, which I was proud to attend, as it was my grandmother's alma mater. Once I graduated high school, I had a taste of the independence I sought when I was allowed to live alone in an old Victorian house my parents had bought in Pacific Grove. It was undergoing extensive repairs and construction during the summer before I went off to college, but I loved being on my own again.

I started at Colorado State College in Greely,

Sketch of our Victorian house in Pacific Grove. (1968)

Colorado, in the fall of 1964 and left in the spring of 1965. Colorado in the fall was intoxicatingly beautiful—the colors burst more vibrantly than the season in La Jolla or San Carlos ever did. The college had changed a lot since my grandmother's days, I'm guessing. Back then it was known as a teaching college, but by the time I got there, it was a party school. One of the many fraternities would throw a party every Friday, dubbed the Friday Afternoon Club, and I was swept up in the lifestyle. For those over eighteen but under twenty-one, there was the popular 3.2% alcoholic beer that was legal to drink, and I started playing a lot of pool. My roommate that year was the leader of a rock band, and I related the most to his artist friends as well as the newspaper staff and the theater students. My social life was going well, and I was interested in the United World Federalists, but my grades were not especially good, particularly once winter hit. I stayed in Colorado during winter holidays and worked at a ski resort. The beauty of autumn was completely stripped away in winter, leaving the landscape bare, brown, and bleak. Seasonal depression came with the cold, and I fiercely missed living in evergreen Pacific Grove. My grades suffered, and I was not asked to come back for my sophomore year.

CHAPTER

5

Tripping out of San Francisco

The summer of 1964 before college was a crazy, fun, party-filled time of smoking pot for the first time, hanging out, listening to jazz and blues LPs at night. I lived on my own in my parents' 1880 Victorian house in Pacific Grove while extensive remodeling was happening to restore the house to its former Victorian state, and so I had a lot of freedom. I went to the 1964 Monterey Folk Festival before leaving for Colorado State. I was a Joan Baez groupie, and she always looked beautiful every time I saw her as she passed me in her convertible Jaguar XKE. I remember her sounding wonderful, but her guest, Bob Dylan, was screechy and drunk during his set, which disillusioned me a bit about him as an artist. I had first seen Bob Dylan during his solo concert in 1963 at the Berkeley Community Theater, and I had been one his underground followers. I loved his first record, though most my friends thought his voice was too screechy and out-of-tune. Though his performance at the folk festival put me off somewhat, I still appreciated his artistry and the way he inspired so many other artists. I wasn't really a fan of The Beatles in their bubblegum pop stage, but with the release of *Rubber Soul* and after smoking my first marijuana cigarette in 1965, I started to love them, especially John Lennon. They were a part of the movement of new ideas—they were changing with the times, and it was a brave new world.

Anyway, I returned to the Monterey area after dropping out of Colorado State in 1965 and got a job at a golf course in Pebble Beach. I discovered a love of photography and the dark room at this time. Luckily my friend Alan McEwan had a dark room I could use in Carmel, as his father was a professional photographer. My most frequent subject was the Monterey Peninsula, especially Point Lobos and Big Sur.

I frequented jazz clubs in Monterey and San Francisco such as Black Hawk and Jazz Workshop, and it was in such a club, called the Colony Club, that I saw my hero Dizzy Gillespie. He hadn't been at the Monterey

Jazz Festival that year, and I was excited to see him. That night my friend and I met his drummer, the late Candy Finch, and we asked him if he'd like us to show him around the Monterey Peninsula that we loved so much. We knew that, as traveling musicians, they didn't often get to see the areas they visited, and we wanted them to be able to enjoy the beauty of Monterey.

When we showed up at the Saint Charles Hotel where the band was staying, Dizzy Gilliespie was standing there, multiple cameras slung around his neck, with the whole band. We drove Dizzy and his band around the Monterey Peninsula in his Volkswagen bus, the kind with the windows all the way around. We took them down the coast to Carmel and Pacific Gove, where they met my mom. I knew she'd be delighted, and Dizzy told her that her house reminded him of a New York apartment. We were just rabid jazz fans, ecstatic to meet Dizzy and show him around.

Dizzy Gillespie promotional poster.

Jim's mom and Dizzy Gillespie on a jazz cruise. (1984)

I saw Dizzy months later at the Basen Street West jazz club in San Francisco's North Beach, and he was happy to see me. We had a nice reunion backstage. Almost two decades later I represented Dizzy as his booking agent.

It was around this time that my stepfather talked me into joining the Navy reserve in Pacific Grove. He knew that a war in Vietnam was looming, and so wanted me to enlist in the Navy before I could be drafted into the Army and be sent out into the jungles of Southeast Asia.

All this time, I missed San Francisco and wanted to move there. I missed the culture and freedom the city embodied in those days. In the late fifties and early sixties, North Beach was the city's Italian district. It was full of exotic, international, Victorian buildings, jazz clubs, improv theaters, bookstores, and art houses. San Francisco had a small-town feeling, a one-mindedness. We weren't distracted by computers or phones. The entire city was in on it — we all had a community together even though we also had our own smaller communities. Nowadays, San Francisco is more insular than it used to be. That's not to say that all of San Francisco was hip back then, but many of the districts were. It's become less of a place where people can actually live. I had a pride in it—we all did; from the richest to the poorest residents, we all loved our city. I missed it every time I left.

During the summer of 1966 I moved to San Francisco to be a part of The Good Samaritan Episcopal Church, a summer program that set up recreational activities for teenagers who lived in the Sunnydale housing projects and that ran the Hamilton Family Shelter near the Haight-Ashbury, though I'm not sure how much good we did. I was with the diverse group who worked in the Sunnydale housing projects.

We were only there for a summer, and it's hard to make a lasting impact on a community in such a short amount of time. However, any amount of effort to improve the lives of these children was a net positive, and I was proud of the work we did. Everyone who worked together lived in one big funky house, and I heard stories from the people who worked at the shelter about how interesting and groovy the nearby Haight-Ashbury was becoming. There were a lot of characters in the house from all parts of the country, some of whom became my friends. In particular, I was close to Ron Stalling, an alto sax player known as The Rev. He was one of the original members of the San Francisco Mime Troupe, who did radical political shows around the country. The hippie movement was just barely beginning in San Francisco back then, and the strong sense of community it fostered was unlike anything I had found in La Jolla or San Carlos; it barely felt as if we were even part of the greater United States. In fact, San Francisco is often called the most European city in the U.S. I had loved the city since I was twelve, but now I had the opportunity to walk all its hills and explore all its nooks and crannies, taking black-and-white pictures of Chinatown.

These years of my life were spent getting to know both Monterey and San Francisco and building connections with it and its jazz musicians. In the September of 1966, I moved, with The Rev and other musicians, into a pink house in the panhandle of Golden Gate Park. I was interested in new ways of living, then. I smoked pot and dropped acid with my new friends. My first acid trip was with Osley Acid, which is a pure acid made by the guy who also made the acid for The Grateful Dead. My trip lasted three hours, and it was a beautiful experience. I just spent it smiling blissfully at the other people with me, people who were strangers, yet who I felt connected to because of the experience we were all having together. We were all part of a journey to raise our consciousness, and the acid played a key role in opening our minds to new ways of thinking.

While all of this was happening, I still was meeting once a month with the Navy reserve. We took a week-long summer cruise off the coast and a week of boot-camp, and I hated it. After our first meeting back in 1965, I tore my uniform off and left it on the floor. The Navy was not a very good place for a free spirit. Boot camps are an indoctrination period to learn how to act as a group with one mind. I felt suffocated; I hadn't known it would be so regimented—I thought I would be going to sea more. I had believed the recruitment officers when they said, "Join the Navy, see the world," but it wasn't true at all—they rarely let their lower enlisted men off the ships, and they discouraged us from experiencing new cultures. It didn't help that I didn't believe in the wars being fought at the time, especially the Vietnam War. My parents told me that every experience has value, but I disagree. I would have been happy to have never been in the military. Right as I was flourishing in Haight-Ashbury at its height in 1966, everything came tumbling down when I was called up to be in the Navy service full-time.

CHAPTER

6

In the Navy Now

I n the fall of 1966, I had to get my orders. It was a culture clash to come from Haight-Ashbury and go to the Treasure Island Navy base, and it was something of a shock for me. I was assigned to the Naval Air Station on Whidbey Island, which is north of Seattle in the San Juan Islands, just below the Canadian border. The San Juan Island chain has hundreds of islands with beautiful landscapes. They were full of northern rainforests and were beautifully lush in the summer. The northwest is nature's trick—the summer is alive and colorful, but the winter is depressingly black and white. I was assigned to an air squadron and lived a very humdrum experience. I would hitchhike to the college town of Bellingham, which was the most happening place near me, and served as my place of sanity away from the Navy. I'd visit GI coffee shops that supported anti-war efforts, and even had an activist girlfriend who lived up there. While in the military, I flew down to San Francisco for a long weekend, during which my friends and I dropped acid. As we were wandering around Golden Gate Park, we happened upon Jimi Hendrix's first show on the west coast, which was in the park for free. It was an incredibly intense experience, but then I had to take three buses, one flight, and then hitchhike my way back to Seattle and the Navy while high on acid. In the airport I remember hearing so many speakers and strange sounds. It's amazing what you do when you're young.

Later I met Brian King, a fellow sailor, in Bellingham and in him found a kindred spirit that also hated the Navy. We would drive up to Vancouver, Canada, for its night life and drive back to the base in the early morning. We had a huge clunker Dodge that was ready to break down at any minute and had push buttons for forward and reverse. We would drive to Deception Pass and listen to soul or jazz music, which had the same effect as drinking a beer—the music would let us mentally recharge and transport our consciousness away from the Navy.

Unfortunately, it ended when a young Navy seaman ratted us out for smoking weed. The CID officer (which is like the FBI), acting on his own, entrapped me

Jim in the Navy on shore leave in Sasebo, Japan, shortly after the *USS Pueblo* incident. (1967)

into feeling comfortable and implicating myself—he offered me food and drinks, befriended me, and told me he just wanted to know the truth about what Brian and I had been doing. Being a naïve hippie, I told him that we hadn't been selling marijuana to the military-dependent teenagers nearby, as the Navy seemed to think, just smoking it ourselves. Back then, people thought pot was as bad as heroin, that it was a gateway drug. In January 1967, there was, for me and Brian, a special court-martial, which was the second-most severe punishment possible in the Navy.

My parents came up for the trial, along with my uncle Ben, then a rear-admiral in the Navy. I had a young Navy lawyer, and I got four months of hard labor in the Navy prison. This included buffing floors, moving rocks around, etc. Prisoners were sent to do labor at different bases around Seattle. Most of the prisoners I knew didn't do horrible things, they just couldn't conform to the military demands. I thought they were cool. All I wanted during this time was to rest and be free. You can't truly appreciate freedom until it is taken away. We could see civilian houses from the prison, and we all yearned to live freely like that again. After three months, I was released because my uncle Ben had made an appeal for a one-month reduction to my sentence.

I went back to the same squadron, with a demotion, and started a new job cleaning everything. I didn't mind this job; I thought it honest. Then there was a bombing

In the Philippines. Jim is at the center, in dark glasses. (1968)

range in Fallon, Nevada, and I was sent to clean the barracks. One night, while hitchhiking back to the base from Reno, I was picked up by some country western musicians who also loved jazz, which was not uncommon. I was sent back to Whidbey Island for a bit, and then sent to personnel school in San Diego.

I got a desk job doing personnel paperwork. It seemed like an incongruous step when, just a few months earlier, I had been court-martialed and put in prison. It made me wonder what the whole thing was about. I didn't mind the paperwork job, though I preferred physical work, but every day I feared getting orders to go to

Vietnam. With only eleven months left in the Navy, my orders came.

It was mid 1967 when I was sent to Vietnam. I was on the USS Ranger aircraft carrier with 5,000 other men and had a huge moral dilemma. I didn't believe in the war at all, but I wasn't sure I was ready to spend three years in prison for resisting. Knowing I had less than a year left in the military, I decided to stick it out. Fortunately, I found other antiwar people. I estimate about a tenth of the sailors on that ship were against the war. I and these others were often tempted to jump ship, and we certainly could have. The ship was enormous, even city-like, and in the dim glow of the war-zone red lights at night, it would be easy to disappear and not be found by superiors on the ship. Japan had a big support system for deserting sailors, but those men often were sent through Russia and on to Sweden or elsewhere, and would never be able to return to the United States.

Instead, I just focused on my seven-month sentence and thought of the light at the end of the tunnel rather than the morally repugnant actions of the aircrafts bombing Vietnam daily. Crossing the Pacific that year, we encountered big winter storms that made for rough crossing at times. For the most part, our schedule was to go to Vietnam for thirty days, then go back to the Philippines for another thirty days before returning to Vietnam.

I was interested in the cultures of the Far East, and I remember smoking DMT at a Shinto shrine upon arriving

On the *USS Ranger* out of Alameda and off of Vietnam —
Mark, Ray, Jim. (1966)

in Japan. DMT was sort of like opium—very strong and smoked through a little pipe. In 1967, Japan was still very old and mysterious. Later, our ship got caught up in the *USS Pueblo* crisis with North Korea (*USS Pueblo* was an American spy ship), and in wartime, there were always Russian ships with nuclear weapons, as well as the American ships. During this crisis, we were at sea without going to port for sixty-six days, thirty days in warm and stormy seas by Vietnam and thirty days in the Artic temperatures of the northern Sea of Japan. Tensions among the crew were running high. For the first time, I found myself thankful for politicians trying to decelerate the situation. If it had been up to the sailors on my ship, we would have just bombed North Korea to "get our guys out."

Finally, after sixty-six days, we pulled into a port in Sasebo, Japan, and I was able to meet up with a friend in Japan, for the first time in a long while. Sasebo is in the southern part of Japan, with hills that reminded me of San Francisco and few great jazz clubs. Not too long after that, my stint with the Navy was up, and I was finally able to go home.

CHAPTER

7

Off to Work

The military had been a terrible experience. I got out in May of 1968—three months early because I applied for the G.I. Bill. In May 1968, I enrolled in Monterey Peninsula College for the summer. I had a professor who liked to smoke pot a lot, and we got along well. After the course was over, I traveled with this professor to Oaxaca, Mexico, with some of his friends. They were anthropologists from Stanford studying the Zapotec Indian religious ceremonies. It was a liberating time for me—I was finally out of the military, and my professor was happy to smoke pot with me.

I left the professor in Oaxaca and decided to go on a bus trip with a gal I met in Oaxaca. We went up to the Techucan spring water plant, then northeast toward the mountains of Teotitlán del Valle, a farmworking community. We slept in a very rundown hotel, and at 5:30 a.m. we caught a bus that disappeared deeper into the mountains and jungle. The other passengers were campesinos, who were often drunk and blasted the radio the entire journey. As we went deeper, the bus stops changed to white stucco A-frames, almost like Swiss chalets.

We were stared at, as the people who lived there didn't often see white people, and the prices of everything changed from pesos to centavos. We got off at one stop called Tierra de Fuego, where we were immediately greeted by a long-haired, constantly stoned Mexican hippie who introduced himself as Ricardo.

He chatted about himself, telling us how he was from Mexico City originally, but was banned from the city after he tore down a statue. He told us about the magic mushrooms that grew nearby, and of a place we could stay. We followed him up a little winding path into the mountains to a mud hut that he offered us for the duration of our trip. He went down to the river where the mushrooms grew and brought some back to us, along with cans of condensed milk to offset the metallic taste of the psilocybin mushrooms.

After I ate about fourteen of the mushrooms, it began raining outside the hut as we got higher and higher.

It was a little scary, because the day before the Federales had confiscated the American cars in the mountainous area and sent a bunch of high Americans back to Mexico City. We had constant drunk visitors at the hut speaking Zapoteca, which none of us spoke. There was a couple from Louisiana in the hut with us who were having a very paranoid high, which made it all a little weird.

Luckily for me, things eventually mellowed out. It had been like an express train to the sky while the mushrooms began affecting me, but once it plateaued, I felt fine. After the rain stopped, the clouds parted to reveal the beautiful moon, and the nirvanic peace promoted a euphoria in me.

The next morning, Ricardo brought us to a little store where we ate and drank mescal. Then we decided it was probably a good idea to leave the area, given the arrests of American tourists nearby. I had met a Mexican couple in the magic mushroom hut who had an apartment in Mexico City, so I went back to the capital to stay with them.

Their apartment was painted all black, with zodiac signs painted on the walls. I only stayed for a night before moving on again, this time to Acapulco. I checked into a cheap hotel there; at night when I turned on the bathroom light, I saw roaches rush toward the drains by the dozens.

Then I hitchhiked with a friendly couple named Klaus and Sandra, who took me all the way from Acapulco to San Francisco. It was pretty amazing that I was able to get all the way from Acapulco to San Francisco with just one ride.

Once back in the U.S. at the Monterey Peninsula College, I opened up a small anti-war organization (providing draft counseling) to educate young people and encourage them not to join the military. I was once again living in my parents' Victorian house in Pacific Grove when I finished my studies at Monterey Peninsula College and was able to transfer to San Francisco State University during the winter semester of 1969. I was now a junior student, and I was beginning to have my doubts about being in college. I wanted to get out and see the real world. I liked the campus—it was almost an extension of Haight-Ashbury in its new ways of thinking. I was studying the liberal arts, but it didn't feel like a worthwhile pursuit because it was not the real world.

It was a very turbulent time in so many ways—there were the third-world riots going on, and students from SFSU were banned from rallying. Students would rally anyway, and then cops would come and crack people's heads open with their batons. There was always violence in the air in those years. I then worked as a longshoreman and was able to get into the warehouseman's union. We unloaded and loaded ships, and I loved this work. I was happiest doing physical work with a beautiful view to enjoy and was very disappointed to not be able to work full-time. There were about 1,000 full-time jobs available but about 20,000 applicants. I was tempted to join the Merchant Marines because I missed the spiritual experience of being on the sea for days at a time, but I was worried I'd become addicted to a life at sea and not see my family for long periods at a time. I worked as a longshoreman for one year before I had to move on.

While I was working as a longshoreman, I volunteered at the United Farm Workers Union office in San Francisco. The UFW did many things—they made their own credit union for seasonal workers to get low-cost loans during the off-seasons and they built Agbayani Village for retired bachelor Filipino farmworkers to live out their years; it included a soup kitchen, gas station, etc. The National Farm Workers Service Center was the nonprofit side of the UFW, and it did many wonderful things, including providing medical help for workers affected by pesticide poisoning, which the UFW was protesting and lobbying against.

During this period in 1969, I and others were arrested and put in jail for using loudspeakers to announce the International Boycott Safeway Day. The week prior, the Black Panthers had used loudspeakers attached to cars to announce their own events, but they swore at the cops while doing so. The police were very angry, and thus we were arrested. We were in jail with Los Siete de la Raza, who were accused of killing a cop. It was a scary time—there were many murders. I was still going to school full time, but I found fulfillment with the United Farm Workers.

In 1969 the headquarters of the United Farm Workers was in a rundown tuberculosis sanitarium in Kern County. To this day, every time I go down to Delano, I feel like I'm stepping forty years back in time. I volunteered with the San Francisco Union Farm Workers Boycott Office, where I helped with marches, protests, etc. After a few months, I gravitated toward organizing events; combined with my love of music, this turned into my organizing a benefit concert for the union, as described in the first chapter. In October of 1969, Santana headlined along with Mike Bloomfield and Friends. It was right after Santana had released their first album, so they were able to draw a huge crowd. I had planned the concert to be at the Fillmore in San Francisco, and easily a thousand people showed up. Thus, my first concert benefit was very successful in bringing in money for the union.

The union gave us $10 dollars a week pay and $5 for food, which was generous, but not always enough. When it was harvesting season, I went up to Washington to pick apples, and then cherries and apricots in Oregon, and I was able to make enough money for the year. To be a part of the union felt like being part of a family that stretched across the U.S. Unfortunately, the California Farm Bureau was becoming more like the John Birch Society of the fifties and sixties—a powerful, right-wing group. The union was fighting against big agriculture, not little family farmers, and was very international as far as its members went. The Filipinos, being very abused, were the first to go on strike, but there were also black workers, Yemen workers, Arab workers, and even Okies. We picketed the big Safeway—not only a retailer of grapes, but also a grower. Safeway owned Del Monte foods and was responsible for many of the injustices the farm workers faced at the time. Nixon, who was president during this period, was supported by the Teamsters, and he and the Department of Defense sided with the growers. The United Farm Workers was like a guerrilla army, picketing every Safeway in the nation, as well as the owner's mansion. Cesar went on a hunger strike of over 30 days, and the Roman Catholic Church supported the boycott. It was all very dramatic, and fully caught the attention of the nation.

I was living in San Francisco during all this, working part time as a longshoreman, and part time for the United Farm Workers. I felt that there was more to see in the world and was not ready to settle into a career just yet. After just a year with the United Farm Workers Union, I decided to leave union work and my longshoreman job for a while.

CHAPTER

8

Finding Life's Purpose

worked at the Crown Zellerbach warehouse for as long as I could stand the graveyard shift (12 a.m. to 8 a.m.) after leaving the United Farm Workers Union and my job with the longshoremen. I was in the warehouseman's union. The money was good, but I'm not a night person. My sister Vicky lived on the McKenzie River in Oregon, east of Eugene, and I went up to stay with her and to pick cherries. I had picked cherries before, so the work was familiar, and I enjoyed it.

I, my dog Liba, my sister's boyfriend Howard, and some of my sister's friends all slept in a hippie camper along the Columbia River. We made a little encampment

Jim, Vicky, and Howard on the Meckenzie River. (1970)

with our cars circled round to make a common area where we'd pick the cherries. We would spend the nights laughing and talking together after a long day of work in 100-degree heat. The money wasn't very good—I could earn about $1.25 for a bucket of cherries, which meant about $12 a day unless you were very good at it.

When the cherry season ended in midsummer of 1970, my sister, her boyfriend, my dog, and I went up to Hammond, Oregon, to the canneries to find work. I was able to rent a very old Victorian house near Astoria, which is where I sailed through on *The Destiny* many years before. The farmers had big fishing boats with which they'd fish expensive albacore tuna for forty days straight each year, and they always had work for anyone willing to help.

Howard and I hauled blocks of ice and emptied out the hulls of the boats of the albacore tuna while Vicky worked the line canning the tuna. Once we unloaded the tuna from the fishing boats, we packed semis with ice and fish before the truck drivers would drive it all down to the canneries in LA. It was wonderful vigorous work in one of the most beautiful places in the world, and I was happy.

The season ended and we moved to northeastern Washington, to Wantachee, which is known as the apple capital of the world, near Lake Chelan. There the three of us and my dog picked apples. A lot of people came up to pick apples in Washington during the season, especially Okies. If you had the method down, you could make enough money to tide you over for the rest of the year.

The trick was to limit the amount of times you had to position the ladder, then grab three or so apples in one flowing motion into the basket. That way you'd conserve energy and be able to pick longer and faster. You could make ten to twelve dollars per bin, which would add up if you were fast. Also helpful was that in Washington, farms were legally requred to provide living quarters for their seasonal workers. It would be a single room with a poky little kitchen and sitting area, with water and electricity included. We were fairly comfortable, as I slept in the Volkswagen bus with my dog and my sister and her boyfriend slept in the provided accommodations. We had a juicer, so we constantly drank fresh apple juice.

My very good friend Margo, who I had previously met in Zihuantanejo, Mexico, came up to pick apples with us. She was originally from Florida, but she lived in Mexico and could come up to the States to work seasonal jobs to save her money for the rest of the year.

She was a very beautiful woman who had been the assistant to the producer and right-hand on the film *The Shoes of the Fisherman,* with Anthony Quinn. She had dated lots of celebrities, including Frank Sinatra, before her life was changed by a car accident while she was on vacation in Acapulco. After the accident, she left the Hollywood life behind, left all her designer clothing and dates with famous men, and moved to Zihuantanejo. There she built a palapa on the beach and lived out her life. Later on, she had two children, both born in hammocks on the beach by her palapa.

When the picking season was over, I drove Margo to a very famous commune in southern Oregon, where I dropped her off on my journey down to San Francisco. My hippie friends Bill and Karen Shuman had moved to Maui to raise their young children and had invited to me to join them. They lived out in the rural areas of Maui and worked there in service of the Native Hawaiian population.

Things didn't work out for me in Hawaii, however. Bill and Karen were trying to become "perfect beings" while feeding Native Hawaiians. The idea was to follow the pure karmic path and change the world while living in paradise. However, the program was being overrun by hippies coming in to help, but who ended up steamrolling over the voices of those they were supposed to be aiding, and attempting to impose their hippie values on the Native Hawaiian population.

The program was eventually shut down by a superior pastor in the Pentecostal church for not adhering to traditional Hawaiian Pentecostal values anymore. The pastor was from Oahu, and she heard about the Shumans and others giving free food and clothes to those who came to their spiritual services. This pastor had a rigid, narrow-minded idea of religion and spirituality, and so gave orders to the pastor under her, who was on Maui, to put an end to the Shumans' services. By the time I got to Hawaii, the food program was pretty much shut down.

I was trying to figure out what was next for me, so I volunteered to feed terminally ill patients on the island. Bill and Karen, since they could no longer feed people, spent their time reading spiritual texts and creating a lifestyle plan for themselves to live their "best lives." I wasn't ready for the type of lifestyle Bill and Karen espoused. It seemed to me to be a kind of middle-age hippie life, full of narcissism. They were all white people living on

Jim. (1972)

the Native land of Hawaii, producing families in a com-
mune-type living situation and attempting to "get back
to nature" by way of spiritual exploration and a "perfect" diet, which meant eating mucus-less foods. It was
all incredibly self-indulgent.

While I was living there, my mother often spoke
to me about returning to the United Farm Workers. The
1965 march to Sacramento had had a large impact on
my parents and myself, and in 1970 they often urged
me to help the UFW with their boycott and were themselves involved. While I was trying to figure out what to
do with my life, my mother sent me Jon Lewis's book

of photographs documenting the United Farm Workers' protests and strikes.

The pictures in the book really moved me, and it was the final piece that convinced me to leave Hawaii and to once again work for the United Farm Workers. Jon Lewis was a photographer for the UFW, and seeing his work again drove home how much I missed being a part of the union, doing good. I didn't know then, but this decision was the beginning of a six-year commitment to the UFW and La Causa that would change my life as I described in the opening chapter of this book.

CHAPTER
9

Cassell/Cibrian Presents

When I left the farm workers after my six-year involvement, I stayed in Berkeley working at a French Moroccan seafood restaurant washing dishes, cleaning trash, and hauling firewood down from the Sierras. It was a cheap, kind of dirty place, and the chef was a semi-alcoholic who liked to party more than work, but it was good to live a simple life again. Eventually, however, I was convinced by my friends who had helped me

Jim, former business partner Al Evers and McCoy Tyner at the Great American Music Hall, SF, mid-1980s.

put on benefits before to return to doing shows. This time, I did commercial shows, which was a completely different scene. The biggest commercial promoter in those days was Bill Graham, who had a monopoly on all the best bands. I did all the kinds of music Graham didn't do: jazz, Latin jazz, blues, Puerto Rican salsa, and Tex-Mex. It was risky at times—the music business was competitive and attracted sleazy people who wanted to make a lot of money.

Over two years of doing shows on my own, I joined with my other partners, Al Evers and Abel Cibrian, to create our company Cassell/Cibrian Presents. Our logo was a beautiful parrot. Al helped us by providing the money to front the shows, and we paid him back later on. We were young and didn't know that we should have gotten loans and investors instead, but Al was reimbursed in the end.

We wanted our first show to be important, so we decided to set up an annual Cinco de Mayo show at the Greek Theater in Berkeley. The Greek has a long history of significant shows and has a beautiful sloping views down to the San Francisco Bay. We tried to exemplify what the Bay Area was all about: inclusivity, especially of all races and creeds.

Our first show was sold out at 8,000 people, and we were able to book Ray Barreto, Salsa Orchestra from New York, Cal Tjader, Mongo Santamaria, Airto from Brazil, and Luis Gasca and Friends. We booked shows that were soul combined with salsa, with Tito Puente and the Tower of Power, Little Joe y la Familia, Eddie Palmieri, Pete Escovedo, Gato Barbieri, Stanley Turrentine, Sheila E., Cal Tjader, and all the other musicians in the Bay Area that were into Latin rock and jazz. We were becoming known for putting on exciting concerts, and they attracted all kinds of people, even high-profile ones like Santana and his brother Jorge, who wanted to be a part of the happening scene we were creating. I was starting to really make my way into Latin jazz and Brazilian music.

Sometimes, though, it was difficult working with artists. We booked a show with Eddie Palmieri, the Mongo Santamaria Band, and some others, with Eddie being the major draw. Mongo wanted to be co-billed with Eddie, even though it was clear that Eddie was the headliner. On the day of the concert, Mongo tried to close the show down with the excuse that his trumpet player hadn't showed up. This was an issue not only because we had budgeted the time to have all the artists perform, but also because Mongo could have incited a riot by not performing.

Eddie appeased Mongo by agreeing to go second-to-last instead of last, the way a headliner is meant to. Mongo miraculously found his trumpet player and was slotted to play last in the traditional headliner spot. It didn't work out very well for Mongo in the end, as Eddie put on a very good show, and people left while Mongo Santamaria was playing the final slot. I never forgot Mongo's bad behavior, recklessly putting our show and business at risk because of his pride.

It was a difficult business to be in, not just because of the occasional artistic ego. As a business, Cassell-Cibrian Presents was basically breaking even. We used our own money most of the time, with little help from investors. When a show didn't do well and lost us money, we were personally financially hurt.

One such concert was our 1976 Cinco de Mayo show, which was rained out. We had spent all our money booking Machito and some other groups, as well as getting the venue and everything set up, so there was a lot to lose. The show that lost us the most amount of money, however, was the December 10th, 1977, show

Jim at The UC Greek Theatre for Cassell/Cibrian productions.

at the San Francisco Civic Auditorium. We had booked Johnny Pacheco and the Ray Barretto orchestras, but we only drew about 1,000 of the predicted 8,000 crowd. The next day, we had booked the same groups to play at the Hollywood Palladium, which sold similarly.

The promoting business is basically a crapshoot, but we learned a hard lesson that day: most Latinos couldn't afford to go to a show in early December. In our line of work, we had to pay everyone else before we paid ourselves, and sometimes we fell right on our faces. Those two shows lost us about $20,000.

We worked in the commercial promoting business for three to four years before Al and I decided we were done. Al had lost some money, and we both wanted a

**Ray Barreto in a commercial concert at the
Greek Theater, Berkeley. (1977)**

regular paycheck. Al and I kept in touch, and we took a
job together at a club called Christo's in San Francisco
where we booked national jazz names to come and perform, then did the publicity for those performances.

Christo's was in a beautiful historical building in
downtown San Francisco where the downstairs was
a topless dance floor and the upstairs was a jazz club.
Christo, the owner, was a Greek immigrant who didn't

Greek Theater concert, Berkeley. (1978)

know anything about putting on shows, but luckily, I was very adept by this point. It was difficult, though, because even here there was a monopoly to work around. Jack Whitmore controlled the whole market from where he lived in New York. He represented all the big groups and booked them into Keystone Korner, which was owned by Todd Barken. Whitmore refused to work with me at all.

I was able to get great jazz names anyway, like Cal

One of the agency's last shows. (1978)

Tjader, Willy Bobo, Jimmy Witherspoon, The LA Four,
Lourindo Almadea, Bill Summers, Frank Rosolino,
Eddie Jefferson, Sonny Stitt, and Richie Cole—in part

because of the work I had done earlier with the United Farm Workers, and the efforts I had made to establish myself in the Bay Area jazz scene.

CHRISTO'S

445 Powell Street
San Francisco 94102
982-7321

Jazz Cabaret presents

The Top Names in Jazz!

Tuesday, April 4	★ KWAKU DADEY & THE AFRICAN HERITAGE
April 5-8 Wed.-Sat.	**EDDIE JEFFERSON/ RICHIE COLE** ★
Tuesday, April 11	ART LANDE & FRIENDS ★
April 12-15 Wed.-Sat.	★ **MILT JACKSON**
Tuesday, April 18	SMITH & GAIL DOBSON & TRIO ★
April 19-22 Wed.-Sat.	★ **PEPPER ADAMS**
Tuesday, April 25	ART LANDE & FRIENDS ★
April 26-29 Wed.-Sat.	★ **THE L.A. FOUR:** RAY BROWN, LAURINDO ALMEIDA, BUD SHANK, JEFF HAMILTON ★

COMING: WILLIE BOBO, HAROLD LAND/BLUE MITCHELL, EDDIE HENDERSON!

Limited Seating • Advance Tickets at all BASS OUTLETS or DIAL T•E•L•E•T•I•X•

Jazz club flyer. (1978)

CHAPTER
10

The Berkeley Agency

Al and I had worked at Christo's for a year before we tired of the job. Around then, Christo decided he wasn't making enough money booking jazz artists and decided to branch out and book country western artists instead. He changed the name to JR's, after the name of a character in a popular television show, *Dallas.* He kept the downstairs a sleazy topless bar. While contacting jazz artists to play at the club, Al and I had met many artists who wanted representation. This gave us the idea to start The Berkeley Agency, a talent and music booking agency, in 1978. Our office was at Telegraph Avenue and Channing Street, where many infamous protests had taken place. Even my desk was historical—it had previously belonged to Eldridge Cleaver of the Black Panthers. Al wasn't very interested in booking artists; he wanted to manage artists and do projects. I did the majority of the booking, calling, faxing, endorsing record sales, etc., kind of groundwork of running an agency, because my artists expected me to get them jobs and income.

We'd get the commission for dates seven to thirteen months after they were booked, so it was important to properly balance our finances. Al eventually departed the agency after about a year and a half and took a job at Palo Alto Records, which had just opened, and we continue to have a good relationship to this day.

Most of the artists who contracted with The Berkeley Agency discovered us by word of mouth from the many musicians I had met over the years, especially from my days putting on benefits for the United Farm Workers. I had also built a reputation by doing commercial shows. I wanted artists who already had some kind of following and direction for their careers, but mostly I wanted musically talented artists who were doing something interesting and worthwhile with their art.

There's a lot to choosing who to represent; you need to have a good ear for whose personality and

SOURDOUGH ▬

What's the craziest thing you've seen in show business?

(as asked of talent agents and managers)

Jim Cassell, President of The Berkeley Agency (represents Dizzy Gillespie, Pete Escovedo, Paul Horn, Joe Williams)

About six or seven years ago we had 5,000 people at the Telluride Jazz Festival (12,000 feet up in the Colorado mountains near the Four Corners area). There were twelve inches of rain over the three-day period—the most rain the area had had in a hundred years. But through it all the most amazing thing happened— people of all ages let their hair down and had a wonderful celebration of music (in the open amphitheater). It was so humid, steam was coming off the silhouetted figure of piano player Cecil Taylor. It was pouring when Gil Scott Heron spoke to the crowd about getting rid of the rain and then *—Mark Gordon* stopped.

marketability will grow best with your partnership, and a good eye for picking out stage presence and chemistry.

I represented Cal Tjader, Richie Cole, Art Pepper, and the late and great Eddie Jefferson. I was excited to work with Eddie Jefferson, one of the originators of scat jazz singing, who had recently partnered up with Richie Cole, an alto sax player. Tragically, however, Eddie was killed at one of the venues where I had booked him, a club in Detroit called Baker's Keyboard. A previous friend was jealous of the new fame Eddie was earning, so this past friend shot him with a shotgun after Eddie's show as he was leaving.

Eddie was a sweet human being, who was always upbeat and humble. Richie Cole had looked up to Eddie Jefferson as a father figure and was completely torn up by his death.

I managed Richie and his band, Alto Madness, for ten years after that. I booked him at the Playboy Jazz Festival, the Monterey Jazz Festival, and many others. We were able to get a very good headline in the San Francisco newspapers that said, "Riche King Cole Rules Monterey Jazz Festival." He played five performances over three days with his own band, as a soloist, with The Manhattan Transfer, with Lionel Hampton and his band, and with others.

Both Richie and I believed in the jazz message of honesty and improvisation in music. He delivered on that belief to his fans with a fun humor, which is why

Richie Cole's Japan tour. (1981)

he did well with his swinging bebop. It was a magical time in his career, and I took pride in helping it make it all happen. All our hard work over the first two or three years of our business relationship and friendship was starting to pay off. Many of his fans didn't speak English, but jazz is a universal language. He had an especially big following in Japan, and toured there as well as appearing on Japanese TV and radio shows. His fans were enamored with his gifted playing style and young, fun take on bebop. His band was always hot, the chemistry was always hot. Paired with his humor, Richie had an amazing image and presence. Image is very important in the Japanese music industry, sometimes more than the quality of the music. Richie had a very good stage presence and image, so he did very well in Japan for many years.

In 1983, during the Cold War, Sr. Habierno from the Plaza Jazz Festival in Cuba heard of Richie Cole and his New York band and invited them to play at the jazz festival that year in Havana, Cuba. I had had an association with Leopold Records in Berkeley, which was the only record label producing Cuban artists in the U.S. at the time. Organizing the trip was very clandestine, as the U.S. government couldn't be involved.

I had an arrogant attitude toward the U.S. policy, and thought it was a big joke that U.S. citizens couldn't travel to Cuba and perform. The FBI did find out about our intentions and snooped around my office, but we were able to go anyway. At that time, I believed in Fidel Castro, who wanted to meet Richie and the band. We almost did meet, but we had to leave the next day, so we didn't have time. The weather was perfect while we were there, lovely and summerish in February. We could pick up American jazz music from radio stations broadcasting from Miami; it was very popular among the Cubans in Havana. I really felt that the Cubans had a lot in common with Americans, certainly more so than other eastern-block countries. After all, our countries are only ninety miles apart.

Cuba airport poster. (1984)

all N. York guys want to do it.

EMBASSY OF THE CZECHOSLOVAK SOCIALIST REPUBLIC

212-834-0925
Chinese Town

CUBAN INTERESTS SECTION

Tel. (202) 797-8518.

2630 16th Street N. W
Wash. D.C. 20009

WASHINGTON, D.C.

December 17th, 1984

Mr. Jim Cassell.
The Berkeley Agency.
2490 Channing Way. Suite 406.
Berkeley, California 94704.

by 12:00
1:15 a.m. Hava.

R. Cole tix
S.F. Cuba. N.Y. S.F.

10. Feb. 13 back Feb. 19th —
11 8-seat pers. p. Cole, Mitchell (Jusey
+ its "Idolita" w. Jano

Dear Mr. Cassell;

I'm please to inform you that the Cuban Agency for the Artists (CUBARTISTA) -
wish to invite you, Mr. Richie Cole and Alto Madness Group, to participated -
in the International Jazz Festival, that will be held in Havana, Cuba, from -
the 14th to the 19th of February 1985.

According with the information from CUBARTISTA, Cuba would be please to covert
all your expenses, including international transportation and 10 cuban pesos
daily to each of you during the stay. The tickets (PTA) will be sent to your
address in order to fly San Francisco-Mexico-Havana and the same way back.
The exact date for the trips shall be February 11th (to Cuba) and February --
22nd (back to the U.S.), because the time-table of the Airways Companies.
Regarding with the Jazz Festival, it was created in 1980 with the participa--
tion of figures as Tania Maria from Brazil, Duo Docu Leczi from Czechoslovak,
and Ronnie Scoth from Great Britain, etc.
In 1985 will be among others renowned figures Tete Monteliou from Spain, Dave
Valentin from USA, Sven Bergerntz, and from Cuba; Arturo Sandoval and his Group,
Irakere, etc, and of course "Richie Cole and Alto Madness".
Mr. Cole is invited to realize 4 performances in an open place.
I'll appreciate very much if you could sent me as soon as possible the passport
information on all the people.
On the 2 weeks before the date of departure, I'll also need those passports in
order to stamp the visas.
Thank you for your kind attention and please do not hesitate to contact me -
by phone or letter if you feel it necessary.

Cuban Airlines
Mexican Airlines
800 - 531-7921

Sincerely,

Alina

Bring Passport! don't
Send b ✓

B. Abierno
Cultural Affairs.

Cuba correspondence. (1984)

THE BERKELEY AGENCY

2490 CHANNING WAY, SUITE 406, BERKELEY, CA 94704
TEL (415) 843-4902

*return~ 18th~ Ed, Victor &
Keith Snowdes*

OK

DEC. 27, 1984

SENOR B. ABIERNO
CULTURAL AFFAIRS
CUBAN EMBASSY
2639 16th Street N.W.
WASHINGTON D.C. 20009

*cant go to cuba~
Vic Juris~*

Dear Senor B. Abierno;

I received your letter and here is the imformation which you need
to make this tour succeed for the RICHIE COLE/ALTO MADNESS group.

Most important we can only travel for a certain period of time since
we have other dates we are working, our schedule is:
depart Cuba: **Feb. 13**
return U.S.A.: **Feb. 19th** - *back 18th~*

Ticket imformation:

RICHIE COLE: his ticket should read : San Francisco-Mexico-Havana-
Mexico-New York & back San Francisco

JIM CASSELL: ticket should read: San Francisco-Mexico-Havana-Mexico-San Francisco

VICTOR JONES: ticket should read: New York-Havana-New York
(Drums)

DANNY MIXON: ticket should read: New York-Havana-New York
(piano)

ED HOWARD: ticket should read: New York-Havana-New York

Equipment :   a.) (1) full set of trap drums without cymbals
b.) (1) baby grand piano tuned

JIM CASSELL & RICHIE COLE's tickets should be sent to: BERKELEY AGENCY
2490 CHANNING WAY SUITE 406
BERKELEY, CALIF. 94704

JONES, MIXON & HOWARD tickets be sent to:
ED HOWARD
188 Norfolk #56
New York, N.Y. 10002

* we need a full fare ticket for (1)bass fiddle

Total Tickets: five(5) plus (1) bass fiddle ticket- 6 tickets total

212-475-3450

Cuba correspondence. (1984)

Early on in the agency's time, I was approached by Tito Puente and Johnny Rodriguez, who remembered me from the days when I put on the United Farm Workers benefit concerts. Tito and Latin Jazz Ensemble had just played at the 1980 Montreux Jazz Festival in Switzerland. They wanted me to represent them because I had a reputation for working well with jazz groups and getting artists into performing arts centers around the world, especially ones that wouldn't normally book jazz or Latin jazz musicians.

Tito and his band had been working mostly in the Latin music community, and they were ready to branch out more. Tito was a great arranger and composer, overall an extremely talented man, and it was a pleasure booking him on shows all around the country. One of my accomplishments was having him play two nights with the Los Angeles Philharmonic at the Hollywood Bowl, which sold 26,000 tickets. He had always wanted to play with the Los Angeles Philharmonic—he loved symphonies.

Tito represented that special energy that New York Puerto Ricans had. He grew up in Spanish Harlem, and it seemed like every New York cabdriver and hotel worker knew his name. He made it look like everyone on the west coast was standing still in comparison to him. His Nuyorican energy was contagious. Hardly anyone knew he could play five different instruments.

When he was in his 70s, his doctor said he had

Tito Puente gets his star at the Hollywood walk of fame.
(2000)

Tito Puente, Jim, and Jimmy Frisura. (1986)

lived the life of three people. I was able to sign Tito onto Concord Records, and he won a Grammy later. I was glad to be a part of the history in exposing Tito Puente to his great legacy. I was there when he got his star on Hollywood Boulevard, which was one of the highlights of his careers.

Those early days with the agency were some of the best times I had. I traveled with the bands I represented and was able to meet and build relationships with some of the most influential jazz artists of the time. I believed in my artists and worked hard for them. We really saw the genre grow and change over those years, especially with the meeting and mixing of cultures.

CHAPTER
11

America's Music

 ow we think of jazz as America's only original music, but that wasn't always the case. My whole life, I was on a crusade to get jazz recognized as a distinguished and cultured art form worthy of respect by the stuffy, respected venues that avoided jazz musicians and instead focused on what they considered to be "refined" art, such as ballet and opera. In other words, they only booked European music, nothing indigenous or homegrown in America. Jazz was not just a music genre—it represented a move

Jim's first booth at Western Arts Alliance in Monterey. (1982)

toward freedom of expression and equality.

To that end, I was the first jazz agency to start working with the Western Arts Alliance as well as larger international performing arts centers to help jazz move into other spheres. It wasn't necessarily that audiences of the older venues were uninterested in Jazz; it was more often that the directors of the venues had antiquated ideas of art and treated jazz as the ugly stepchild of music forms.

People liked working with me because I was honest,

**Poncho Sanchez, Dizzy, Gillespie, and Jim
at the Monterey Jazz Festival. (2003)**

knew the music, and didn't overcharge them. Also, I built and kept up good relationships with venue owners by helping them find acts to perform even though they weren't interested in any of my own acts at the time. What was important to me was to promote jazz and the arts, and to be respected for that. Much of the success of my agency was based on the relationship with the buyers, the audiences, and the artists.

115

Al Gore and his wife, Tipper Gore, with Jim after a performance by Poncho Sanchez for the Thelonius Monk Institute held at their home. (1996)

Madeline Albright, Jim, and Poncho Sanchez at
The John F. Kennedy Center for the Performing Arts. (1996)

One such lasting relationship was with Poncho Sanchez, an Afro Cuban, Latin jazz, and salsa musician. Poncho's wife, Stella, and my wife, Valerie, became very good friends over the years. Poncho had a very good record company named Concord Records, and everything was going in our favor.

I spent a lot of time promoting Poncho's image— he was a tough-looking, heavy-set Chicano with a big beard and a braid going down his back. He liked to wear Kangol hats, and we trademarked the special type of conga drums he played called Remo drums, which ended up selling worldwide. In 2000 he won a Grammy for Best Latin Jazz Album and was known for the energy of his shows—his music built up and took off, and the energy in the room was like being in a massive communal party.

Poncho performed at the Kennedy Center for the Thelonius Monk Institute where the honorary chair was Vice President Al Gore and his wife, Tipper Gore. Later, Poncho, Mickey Hart, and Terri Lyne Carrington did the drumroll right before Al Gore announced his intention to run for president.

Poncho even did some tequila ads with Don Julio himself, of Don Julio Tequila. Don Julio was eighty years old at the time, and was very established. Their marketing strategy was to promote the tequila around the release of Poncho's new record as two great legends meeting— Poncho with his Latin Jazz, and Don Julio with his tequila.

These were very exciting times for all of us. We did

big promotions and concerts all over the country with this agreement. Over time, Poncho's established fanbase in Los Angeles grew to international size with his fame, and he essentially had his pick of any artist he wanted to perform and record with, people like Ray Charles, Chic Corea, Freddie Hubbard, Tower of Power, Tito Puente, Celia Cruz, and many more.

Around 2008, a man only known as Fast Eddie invited Poncho to come play for the king of Thailand, an unexpectedly avid fan of Jazz. Fast Eddie had worked with Poncho on a previous project and was now head of the film department of a major production company in Thailand. The king of Thailand had studied in Boston until his cousin, who was then the king, died, and he had to return home to take up the throne. It was his time in America that had introduced jazz to the king, and he brought his love of it home with him. Poncho played at the king's eightieth birthday party at the cultural center in Bangkok.

On the second day he played at a fancy hotel ballroom for a Latin dance. I thought it was kinda corny— like out of the 1950s. On the third day, he was set to play for the king himself. Just before he was picked up for the performance, however, he was told that no women or managers would be allowed to accompany him. Poncho was very disquieted by this last-minute information, and was uncomfortable leaving his wife at the summer palace, which had a hotel where she could stay while Poncho met the king.

I was not allowed to go to the party, but Poncho told me he performed for the king from about ten at night until about eight the next morning. He wasn't required to play every song, and he didn't seem to have enjoyed it much. The king played the saxophone and trumpet with Poncho; when I asked him what he thought of the royal's playing, Poncho said he "sounded like he was on the high school level."

As Poncho grew older, his music became more routine, and lost some of its exciting and innovative spark. During the recession of 2009, his popularity began to flag, as it did for all jazz musicians during that time. Our own relationship became strained, as artists always blame their managers first. I had other deserving artists I was working with and wanted to be appreciated for my work, so Poncho and I parted ways.

I never had contracts with the artists I represented—a contract can't enforce the agency and the artist to work well together, and if things go south, then both parties are trapped in an unhappy situation. There's a natural high when you work well with an artist that makes it a joy to help them grow their careers and to hear their wonderful music evolve.

In 1995, Connie Laventurier came to work for the agency full time. She was my right-hand aide and administrative assistant who handled publicity and many other details. She went to the shows, dealt with the contracts, and worked very hard to fulfill the needs of all the artists.

We worked together until the agency closed.

I went on to work with many other legends in jazz during my years with my agency, including Celia Cruz, James Cotton, Airto and Flora Purin, the Brubeck Brothers, Joe Williams, Toshiko Akiyoshi, Law Tabakin, Art Pepper, Phil Woods, Frank Morgan, La Vay Smith, Steve Lucky, Paul Horn, Eddie Daniels, the Mills Brothers, Tanya Maria, Linda Tillery, Sergio Mendez, and several others. I'll always be honored to have worked with so many amazing artists, and think back very fondly on my time with them until I closed The Berkeley Agency doors in 2016.

My philosophy toward my careers has always been that success happens because you know which artists to choose, you can identify their future potential, and you believe they will achieve it. I didn't do it for the money; it was my passion. If you work hard and do well, the rest follows. It's been an incredible experience that I wouldn't trade for the world.

THE BERKELEY AGENCY has ceased its booking operations after 38 years in the business. Of the move, founder and principal JIM CASSELL said, "I've been fortunate to represent the finest artists in jazz, blues and Latin jazz, and to only represent artists whose music I truly loved and respected. I'm proud of our legacy over the years, working with presenters and agencies to bring our artists to a broader public. It's been a wonderful and fulfilling journey. I'm looking forward to now devoting my experience and energy to personally meaningful mission-driven projects." After producing benefits for Cesar Chavez and the United Farm Worker movement in the 1970s, Cassell translated his experience into commercial concert production. Over the years, his roster included Dizzy Gillespie, Ritchie Cole, Poncho Sanchez and other jazz, Latin jazz and blues legends. Connie Laventurier will continue to serve Berkeley Agency clients and administer contract, venue and artists needs for contracted dates.

From the Fall 2016 issue of INSIDE ARTS.

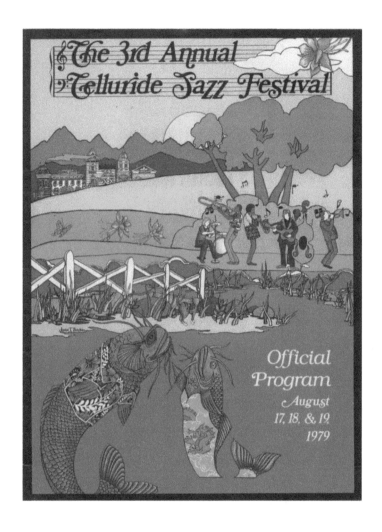

The 3rd Annual Telluride Jazz Festival Program.
Talent booked by Jim's agency. (1979)

Shelia Escovedo and her dad, Pete. They did benefits for the
UFW and also commercial shows with Jim. (1977)

Shelia E. and Flora Purim. (1978)

The late great Eddie Jefferson
at the Russian River Jazz festival. (1981)

Jim and Eddie Razo. (1969)

Jim and Pete Escovedo at the Roosevelt Hotel in Hollywood
at the ceremony for Tito Puente's star on the
Hollywood Walk of Fame. (2000)

Kris Kristofferson and Jim in Stockton, California, at the
Paramount Theater show for the UFW. (2013)

CHAPTER
12

Valerie

I met my wife, Valerie, in 1995 at the Oakland airport as I was coming back from a kayaking trip to Baja California and she was going on the Monterey Jazz Festival At Sea cruise, where three of my bands were booked to play. After seven days of kayaking, sleeping on beaches, and being at one with nature, I joined the cruise, which was going down just south of Tijuana to Ensenada. It was a very different experience, not at all one with nature, but I had an exceptional time getting to know Valerie during those four days. She has a son named Marcelo, who was nine or ten when we met. For a long time, we lived together

Valerie. (1990)

Valerie and Jim, on sailboat in Kauai. (1994)

in the hippie style, meaning we built a home and life together without being married. Fifteen years ago, we decided to get married in a double ceremony with a friend of Valerie's who lives up the street. The ceremony took place on the third day of a rafting trip up the Klamath River, with Valerie's friend's sister performing the service. Around two weeks later, we had a big party on Rodeo Beach to the north of the Golden Gate Bridge. Many of the musicians I had represented came to the wedding as well as our family and our little dog Tito (named after Tito Puente).

Valerie was a musician and had a band called Girl Talk in which she played the lead guitar. They performed jazz, Brazillian jazz, and blues music. She played a Paul Reed Smith guitar like the one Santana uses, as well as the small Brazilian guitar known as the cavaquinho.

The band was respected by the acts I represented, and her positive energy ensured that she got along with almost all the artists she met. I would occasionally get dates for her band, but after 15 years of being in the band, Valerie was burnt out and decided to quit. She took four years off music, but began playing again, and now does lessons. Valerie's third husband and Marcelo's father was from Brazil, so Marcelo always lived in a musical house. He plays the saxophone and likes jazz. Marcelo is now a seventh-grade teacher in Berkeley, where Valerie and I still live. After semi-retiring, I joined the Laney Chorale Choir and received lessons from Lucy Kinchin, a voice coach. The Laney Chorale Choir sang spiritual and classical songs, and we performed at the Paramount Theater in Oakland. Later, Valerie convinced me to join a jazz choir, of which I am still a member. It's now one of my passions; I love the high of performing. Jazz has always been a common denominator in my households—from my mother's house, to the houses I floated around in in my youth, to the home I built with my wife. Jazz always brings the family together, and I believe it is uniquely expressive of the human condition.

Valerie was extremely supportive of my business and was good friends with Stella Sanchez, Poncho Sanchez's wife. She would sometimes come to events and trips with Poncho, Stella, and me. I was established with my agency when we met, and already had some of my best big-name clients. Valerie always encouraged me, not only with managing my booking agency, but also with performing my own music. Over the twenty years we've been together, I've never stopped marveling at how smart, empathic, and creative Valerie is. She became a member of the Berkeley Rotary Club because she was a fan of their philosophies, and is still active with them to this day. She has worked on several of the Rotary Club's projects, including refurbishing schools from top to bottom near the seaside town of Chacala, Mexico. I took Marcelo down there three times to see Valerie while she worked on the project. Later on, I made an eight-day kayaking trip in the Sea of Cortez to Baja

California, where I slept on the beaches and ate fresh seafood every day. I also took a similar trip up in southeast Alaska, where the immense beauty of the landscape maxed me out. I love to be on the sea—over the past twenty years, I've owned three sailboats that I take on long trips, often with Valerie.

My sister Vicky now lives in Eugene, Oregon, and my brother Mike lives in San Diego. The both retired fairly early on in their lives, though Vicky was sort of forced into retirement by the utilities company up in Eugene. She didn't find her life's fulfilment through her career, so I don't think she was overly bothered by this. My parents had died around forty years ago, and I often think of them. It was my parents who prodded me to work for the United Farm Workers, which changed the course of my life. It was my mother who introduced me to jazz. My siblings weren't as interested in jazz as I was, so my mother bonded with me over her love of it. We were very much alike, my mother and me. My stepfather taught me that self-growth, especially growth of empathy, can happen as one grows older. He started out as a strait-laced stockbroker who didn't understand why there were protests and unrest. Then he became a deacon at the Episcopal church, where he expanded his ideas of morality, and later was even jailed for protesting with farm workers. My parents were always very compassionate people— they helped anyone in the community who was struggling. That was the way La Jolla was in my early days—a tight-knit community that supported its families.

I recently took a trip back to La Jolla to celebrate the seventy-second birthday of my friend John Paige. John and I were born two hours apart and have been friends ever since. We would celebrate our birthdays together in the park as we grew up. John still lives in our hometown, so I go and visit him every once in a while. There are many things I love about living in Berkeley—the culture, the history, the hiking trails, the beautiful hills I ride my electric bicycle on—but I miss the beautiful ocean of La Jolla. Every time I go, I take the chance to swim in the ocean when it's warm enough. I get my spirit from the ocean, and it's incredible to simply walk along the cliffs and feel the energy of the ocean in the breeze. It's the most rejuvenating and calming experience I've ever had, and the ocean has and always will be an incredibly important aspect of my life. To be in the ocean's waters is akin to returning to the waters of the womb, to a place before birth. It's where we came from, and it's where we will go.

POSTERS

BUTTONS

FIESTA CAMPESINA

(Program of the First Farm Workers Concert)

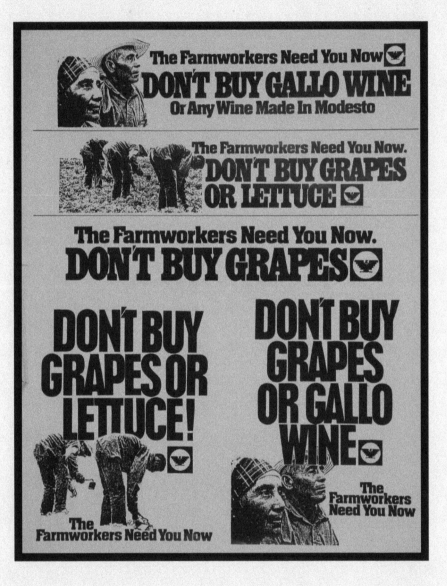

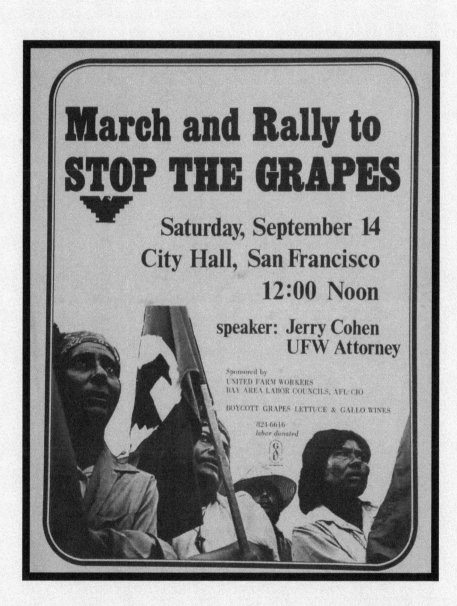

March and Rally to
STOP THE GRAPES

Saturday, September 14
City Hall, San Francisco
12:00 Noon

speaker: Jerry Cohen
UFW Attorney

Sponsored by
UNITED FARM WORKERS
BAY AREA LABOR COUNCILS, AFL-CIO

BOYCOTT GRAPES LETTUCE & GALLO WINES

824-6616
labor donated

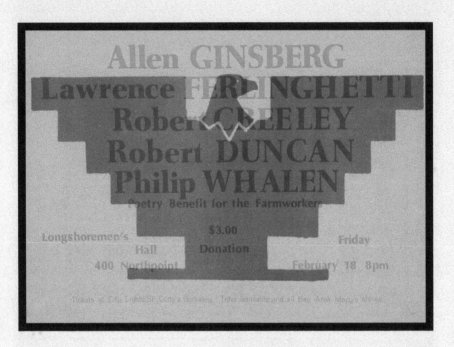

Allen GINSBERG
Lawrence FERLINGHETTI
Robert CREELEY
Robert DUNCAN
Philip WHALEN

Poetry Benefit for the Farmworkers

Longshoremen's Hall
400 Northpoint

$3.00
Donation

Friday
February 18 8pm

Tickets at City Lights SF, Cody's Berkeley , Tides Sausalito and all Bay Area Macy's stores

JOY OF COOKING
Stoneground
Hijos del Sol Teatro

Berkeley Community Theater
Allston & Grove

FRI 28 JAN 8pm
$2.50 In advance   at the door $3.00

Farmworkers Benefit

Tickets — Berkeley Cody's Berkeley SF City Lights Repairs Changes Films and all Bay Area Macy's stores

KRIS KRISTOFFERSON
RITA COOLIDGE

MEChA & A.S. CONCERTS:
CAMPBELL HALL
SAT. NOV. 18
TWO SHOWS 7:30PM & 10:00PM
TICKETS $3.00 ASUCSB & $3.50 OTHERS
MORNINGLORY MUSIC
UCEN INFOR. BOOTH
FARMWORKERS BENEFIT

DANCE CONCERT
U.F.W. Farmworkers Benefit

AZTECA
CAL TJADER LATIN ALL*STARS

BAY AREA JAZZ ENSEMBLE
JON HENDRICKS   ED KELLY
KEN NASH   EDDIE HENDERSON

AND SPECIAL GUEST

* EDDIE PALMIERI *

LONGSHOREMAN'S HALL $4.00 ADV.
Fisherman's Wharf, S.F. $4.50 DOOR
FRI. FEB. 21, 9:00 P.M.
Boycott Gallo Wines!

TICKETS:
SAN FRANCISCO:
CITY LIGHTS BOOKS North Beach
MUSICA LATINA - 2974 & 2388 Mission

OAKLAND:
NEIL THRAMS Bruener's

BERKELEY:
CODY'S BOOKS - Telegraph

AND AT ALL BAY AREA MACY'S AND GREYHOUNDS

DAVID CROSBY & GRAHAM NASH

INVITE THE COMMUNITY TO ATTEND
A TRIBUTE TO THE
PROJECT JONAH &
UNITED FARM WORKERS
SAN FRANCISCO
CIVIC AUDITORIUM
SAT. DECEMBER 14
8:00 P.M.

DESIGN R.TUTEN...

PRODUCED BY STEVEN COHEN, LEO MACKOTA, AND GARY L. JACKSON
SOUND BY ROBERT STERNE OF NORTHWEST SOUND
TICKETS AVAILABLE AT DOWNTOWN CENTER BOX OFFICE, NEIL THRAMS
BOX OFFICE AT BREUNERS AND ALL TICKETRON OUTLETS. PRICES $3.50 · $4.50 · $5.50
FOR FURTHER TICKET INFORMATION PLEASE CALL 788 - 2828
ALL PROCEEDS GO TO PROJECT JONAH & UNITED FARM WORKERS...

RECYCLED PAPER   LABOR DONATED

140

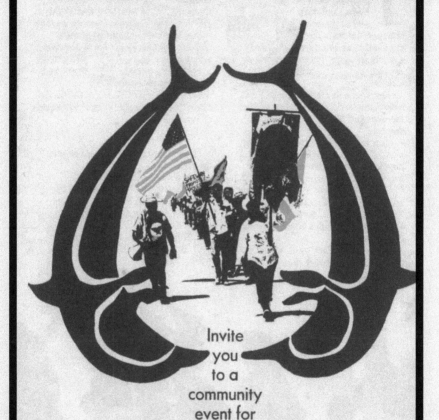

DAVID CROSBY & GRAHAM NASH

Invite
you
to a
community
event for

The Farm Workers and Whales

San Francisco Civic Auditorium,
Saturday, December 14, 1974

All proceeds go to United Farm Workers, Project Jonah and General Whale.

FARMWORKERS CHRISTMAS CONCERT-DINNER
CAL TJADER
LUIS GASCA & friends
featuring **CARLOS SANTANA**
Special Attraction: **MALO**
SUPER LATIN JAM

Friday Dec. 10
Glide Church
330 Ellis
S.F.

8:00
Concert
$2.50

5:30 Dinner $2.50
Bring a can of food

Funds and food from this concert will help make
a better Christmas for children of farmworkers

Tickets: S.F.: City Lights, Outside-In, 2544 Mission   Berkeley: Cody's Books, 845-7852 Or at the door

LITTLE JOE

& THE LATINAIRES

FREE

FIRST 1000
PEOPLE RECEIVE
A FREE
LITTLE JOE
& THE LATINAIRES
RECORD!

8 p.m.
to 1:30

2nd GROUP: LOS ASTROS DEL NORTE

SATURDAY

BAILE OCT. 14

BOYS' CLUB OF STOCKTON

303 Olympic Circle Near King School at Filbert & Marsh

$2.50 in advance • $3.00 at door

ADVANCE TICKETS:

STOCKTON
TICKET OUTLETS:
VALENCIA MUSIC (E. Market St.)
MARIANI'S STORE (S. El Dorado)

VOTE NO ON 22

FREE PARKING

LUIS GASCA & FRIENDS, TOWER OF POWER, MALO, TAJ MAHAL, TEATRO LOS TOPOS, MARIACHI

FIESTA CAMPESINA

SAN JOSE STATE COLLEGE, SPARTAN STADIUM

SUNDAY, JULY 2, 1:00 P.M.
$2.00

FARMWORKERS BENEFIT

TICKETS: SAN JOSE: DISCOUNT RECORDS – VALLEY FAIR · MUSIC BOX – 98 S. 3rd ST. · MUSIC BOX – WESTGATE · SANTA CRUZ : BOOKSHOP SANTA CRUZ ·
SAN FRANCISCO: CITY LIGHTS · BERKELEY: CODY'S · OAKLAND: NEIL THRAMS TICKET AGENCY AT BREUNERS · ALL MACY'S & GREYHOUND OUTLETS (397-3333)

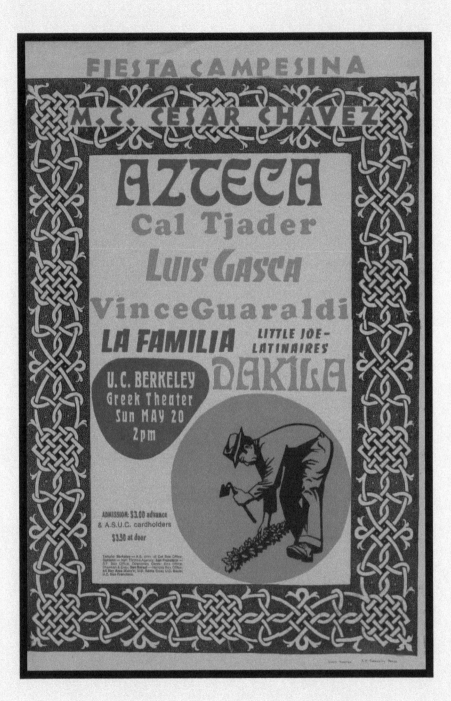

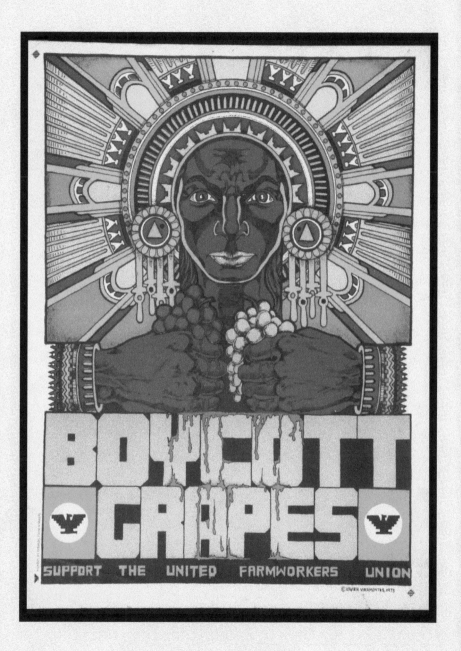

BOYCOTT GRAPES — SUPPORT THE UNITED FARMWORKERS UNION

THIRD ANNUAL
TELLURIDE
Jazz Festival
Saturday
MUSICIAN

1980
STAGE
23rd ANNUAL
MONTEREY JAZZ
FESTIVAL

BOYCOTT
NON-UFW
GRAPES

ÓRALE, HAY TE WATCHO · ZOOT SUIT · BY LUIS VALDEZ · WINTER GARDEN THEATRE ·

JUSTICE FOR FARM WORKERS
NO
ON 22

CLINTON GORE '92
CIRCLE OF FRIENDS

Monterey Jazz Festival
G.O. 1986

THIS CANADIAN CARES
BOYCOTT U.S. GRAPES

DISARMAMENT JUNE 12 HUMAN NEEDS

Monterey Jazz Festival
G.O. 1987

NON-VIOLENT ACTION
UFW AFL-CIO

FIESTA CAMPESINA

Nothing can withstand the force of an idea whose time has come. — *Victor Hugo*

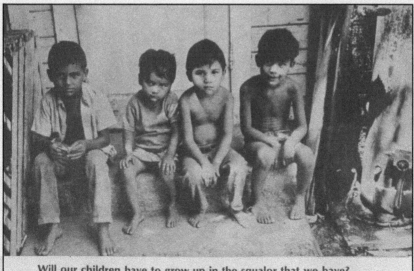

Will our children have to grow up in the squalor that we have?

MALO

BOLA SETE

FARMWORKERS BENEFIT CONCERT
To these performers
who devote
their artistic energies
to LA CAUSA —
OUR DEEPEST GRATITUDE.

Teatro Los Topos
& MARIACHI

LUIS GASCA
& FRIENDS

TAJ MAHAL

TOWER OF POWER

We are tired of back-breaking labor —

With no benefits, no rights to bargain,
no health care.

Let's work to build the Farmworkers' Union.

We need the Farmworkers' Union.

Support our boycotts.

Our sweat and our blood
have fallen on this land
to make other men rich.
Time has come
for liberation.

Que Viva La Causa!

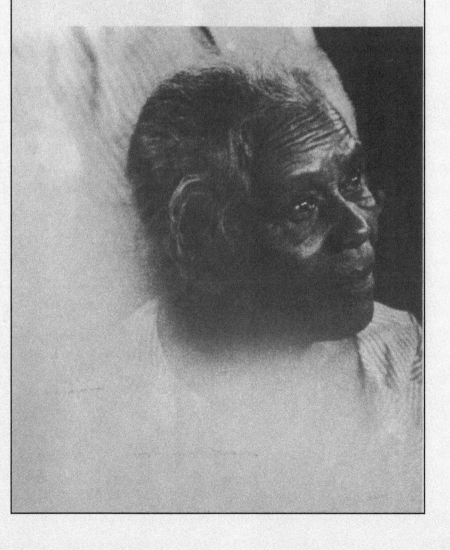

FARMWORKERS CONCERTS

SOUVENIR PROGRAM

SACRAMENTO, CAL EXPO
FRIDAY, JUNE 30th

SAN DIEGO STATE COLLEGE
SATURDAY, JULY 1st

SAN JOSE STATE COLLEGE
SUNDAY, JULY 2nd

UNITED FARMWORKERS

P.O. BOX 62   KEENE, CALIFORNIA 93531